The Seven Continents
Europe

JOANA COSTA KNUFINKE

Children's Press®
An Imprint of Scholastic Inc.

Content Consultant
Jennifer L. Foray, Ph.D., Associate Professor, Purdue University

Library of Congress Cataloging-in-Publication Data
Names: Knufinke, Joana Costa, author.
Title: Europe / by Joana Costa Knufinke.
Description: New York, NY : Children's Press, an imprint of Scholastic Inc., 2019. | Series: A true book |
   Includes index.
Identifiers: LCCN 2018028748| ISBN 9780531128084 (library binding) | ISBN 9780531134160 (pbk.)
Subjects: LCSH: Europe—Juvenile literature.
Classification: LCC D1051 .K68 2019 | DDC 940—dc23
LC record available at https://lccn.loc.gov/2018028748

All rights reserved. Published in 2019 by Children's Press, an imprint of Scholastic Inc.
Printed in North Mankato, MN, USA 113

SCHOLASTIC, CHILDREN'S PRESS, A TRUE BOOK™, and associated logos are trademarks and/or
registered trademarks of Scholastic Inc.

Scholastic Inc., 557 Broadway, New York, NY 10012

1 2 3 4 5 6 7 8 9 10 R 28 27 26 25 24 23 22 21 20 19

Front: Europe
Back: The Parthenon

Find the Truth!

Everything you are about to read is true *except* for one of the sentences on this page.

Which one is **TRUE**?

T or F   Soccer is the most popular sport in Europe.

T or F   The Olympic Games were invented by the Ancient Romans.

Find the answers in this book.

3

Contents

THE BIG TRUTH!

Mountains of Garbage

Karpathos frog

4

Venice, Italy

4 Europe Today

What is life like for people in Europe? **35**

Eiffel Tower

Greenland
(Den.)

ARCTIC
OCEAN

Svalbard
(Norway)

Novaya Zemlya

Moscow, Russi

N
W E
S

Barents Sea

ICELAND

Arctic Circle

Norwegian Sea

RUSSIA

Volga River

Faroe Is. (Denmark)

Shetland Is. (Scotland)

ATLANTIC
OCEAN

North
Sea

SWEDEN

NORWAY

FINLAND

Baltic Sea

Moscow

Scotland

ESTONIA

N. Ireland

IRELAND

UNITED
KINGDOM

LATVIA

DENMARK

Wales

England

NETHERLANDS

RUSSIA

LITHUANIA

BELARUS

Don River

London

GERMANY

Berlin

Jersey (U.K.)

Rhine R.

POLAND

Dnieper River

BELGIUM

Paris

LUX.

LIECH.

CZECH REP.

UKRAINE

Bay of
Biscay

FRANCE

SWITZERLAND

Casp

SLOVAKIA

MOLDOVA

AUSTRIA

HUNGARY

PORTUGAL

ITALY

SLOVENIA

ROMANIA

Danube R.

ANDORRA

MONACO

Corsica
(France)

Madrid

Rome

CROATIA

SERBIA

BOSNIA &
HERZEGOVINA

Black Sea

BULGARIA

TURKEY

SPAIN

Sardinia
(Italy)

MONTENEGRO

MACEDONIA

Majorca (Spain)

KOSOVO

ASIA

Sicily (Italy)

ALBANIA

Athens

AFRICA

MALTA

Crete (Greece)

GREECE

Rhodes (Greece)

Mediterranean Sea

0   200 MI

0   300 KM

Vatican City

6

Continent Close-up

Europe is the second-smallest of

Earth's seven continents. Located entirely in the Northern Hemisphere, it stretches from the Mediterranean Sea in the south to the icy Arctic Circle in the north. Its western side is bordered by the Atlantic Ocean. However, Europe is not completely surrounded by water. The Ural Mountains, which cross Russia from north to south, lie on the eastern side. Europe is actually the western **peninsula** of a huge landmass called Eurasia. Eurasia contains both Europe and Asia, another of the seven continents.

Land area	Just over 4 million square miles (10.4 million square kilometers)
Number of independent countries	At least 50 (five of them with land in Asia)
Estimated population (2017)	About 742 million
Languages spoken	More than 50
Largest country	Russia
Smallest country	Vatican City
Fast fact	Istanbul, Turkey's capital city, has land in both Europe and Asia. The Bosporus is a narrow strait of water between the two continents.

7

Vernazza was founded about 1,000 years ago.

The famous town of Vernazza, Italy, is located along the coast of the Ligurian Sea.

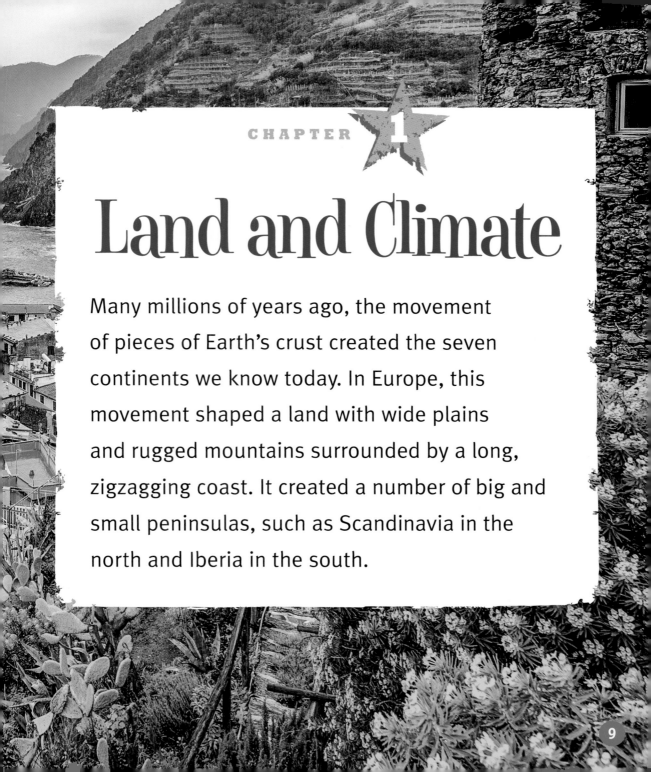

CHAPTER 1

Land and Climate

Many millions of years ago, the movement of pieces of Earth's crust created the seven continents we know today. In Europe, this movement shaped a land with wide plains and rugged mountains surrounded by a long, zigzagging coast. It created a number of big and small peninsulas, such as Scandinavia in the north and Iberia in the south.

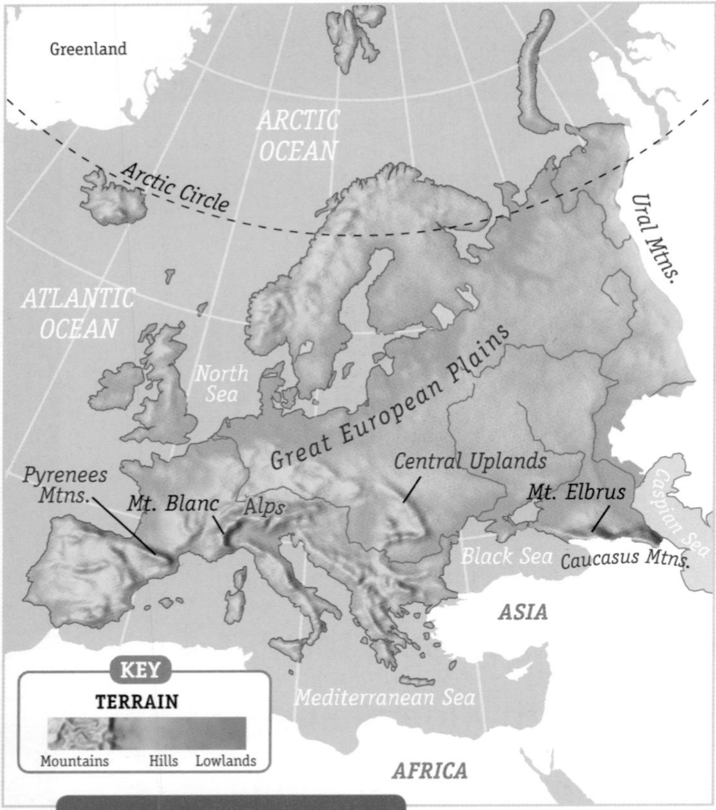
Greenland
ARCTIC OCEAN
Arctic Circle
ATLANTIC OCEAN
North Sea
Ural Mtns.
Great European Plains
Central Uplands
Pyrenees Mtns.
Mt. Blanc
Alps
Mt. Elbrus
Caspian Sea
Black Sea
Caucasus Mtns.
ASIA
KEY
TERRAIN
Mountains
Hills
Lowlands
Mediterranean Sea
AFRICA

This map shows where Europe's higher and lower areas are.

Four Major Landforms

Europe's territory can be divided into four major geographical regions. The northwestern mountains start in western France and stretch along the United Kingdom and Scandinavia all the way to the Urals in Russia. The Great European Plains, the largest region, lie in the center of the continent. They begin in southern France, grow wider toward the northeast, and end in the Urals.

The Central Uplands lie south of the Great European Plains. They begin on the Atlantic coast and run through France and Germany to central Europe. The last of Europe's four main geographical regions is the Alps. This mountian system stretches through central Europe and the Balkan Peninsula. Two tall mountain ranges tower over this area. The Alps separate central and southern Europe. The Caucasus Mountains lie between the Black and Caspian Seas.

More than 80 of the peaks in the Alps reach 13,123 feet (4,000 meters) or higher.

Close and Faraway Islands

Europe also includes thousands of islands and island groups scattered across the ocean. Iceland, for example, lies by itself in the middle of the North Atlantic Ocean. It is a hot spot for geologic activity, including earthquakes, volcanic eruptions, and geysers. The island of Great Britain lies just 21 miles (34 km) off the western coast of France. It is connected to the mainland by an underground tunnel nicknamed the Chunnel.

Greece has more than 2,000 islands, though people live on only about 170 of them.

On the Greek island of Santorini, traditional stone buildings with blue roofs overlook the Aegean Sea.

The Danube is the major waterway in central Europe. It empties into the Black Sea, in the southeastern corner of Europe.

Rivers and Lakes

Many of Europe's rivers can be traveled by boat. They have historically provided a fast and easy means of transportation across the continent. The Volga is Europe's longest river. It begins in the hills near Moscow, Russia, and winds its way south to end in the salty Caspian Sea. Despite its name, the Caspian Sea is actually the world's largest lake. Scattered across the continent are more than 500,000 other natural lakes that are each larger than the average sports field.

What's the Weather Like?

The climate in Europe is milder than it is at the same **latitudes** in other parts of the world. This is because of the Gulf Stream, an ocean current that flows from the southeastern coast of North America toward the North Atlantic Ocean. Thanks to the Gulf Stream, southern Europe enjoys a Mediterranean climate. It has mild winters and warm, dry summers. In central Europe, winters are cold and summers are hot. The northern countries get a lot of rain during fall and winter.

In areas such as Spain's Bardenas Reales, the ground can get so dry that it cracks apart.

RECORD TEMPERATURES

HIGHEST	LOWEST
Athens, Greece; July 1977	Ust' Shchugor, Komi Republic, Russia; December 1978
118°F	−73°F
48°C	−58°C

A Land of Fjords

The northern third of Europe was covered in huge, slow-moving masses of ice called glaciers for millions of years. Over time, **erosion** of the glaciers' ice created deep valleys that filled with seawater, creating fjords. Fjords are deep, narrow **inlets** of sea. There are more than 1,000 fjords along the coast of Norway. Geirangerfjord in southeastern Norway is one of the longest and deepest in the world. Its dark-blue waters and steep mountainsides dotted with waterfalls are natural wonders of breathtaking beauty.

Geirangerfjord is 9.3 miles (15 km) long.

Geirangerfjord can be explored from sightseeing boats or kayaks, as well as by hiking along the rim of its coast.

Polar bears are well suited to life in a cold climate. Their white fur provides camouflage in a world covered in ice and snow.

In winter, the sun barely rises in the tundra. It is not only freezing and windy, but also dark for weeks at a time.

CHAPTER 2

Plants and Animals

A biome is a large geographical area where certain plant and animal species live. These species are all suited to thrive in the biome's climate and geography. Because Europe is so large and its climate is so varied, it has several main biomes. Polar bears and other mammals with thick fur coats make their home in the icy north, while lazy lizards bask in the sun on many islands of the southern Mediterranean Sea.

An Icy World

The northern parts of Russia and Scandinavia are covered by the tundra, a frozen and solitary land. Only low-growing plants such as lichens, mosses, and small grasslike plants can survive in this harsh environment. Reindeer and arctic foxes are two of the few animals able to stay warm there year-round.

The taiga lies south of the tundra. Hemlock, spruce, pine, and other evergreen trees survive in this cold biome. Gray wolves, red foxes, and many species of **migratory** birds make it their home, especially in summer.

A great gray owl flies through a forest in Finland.

Vanishing Forests

Most of the rest of Europe was once covered by forests of oak, elm, birch, lime, and alder. A huge range of plant and animal life once thrived

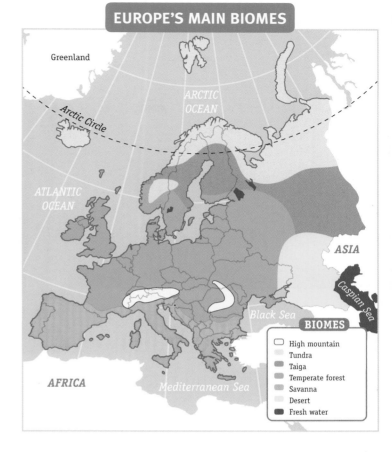

EUROPE'S MAIN BIOMES

Greenland

ARCTIC OCEAN

Arctic Circle

ATLANTIC OCEAN

ASIA

Caspian Sea

Black Sea

BIOMES

○ High mountain
- Tundra
- Taiga
- Temperate forest
- Savanna
- Desert
- Fresh water

AFRICA

Mediterranean Sea

in this biome. However, as people cut down trees for wood and farmland, the forests shrank. Many animals that lived there lost their **habitat**. About 75 percent of the original forests of central Europe have been lost. The trees that remain change color with the seasons and lose their leaves in the fall.

The eggs of the beluga sturgeon, a fish that lives in the Black and Caspian seas, are the world's most prized type of caviar.

Dolphins (pictured), whales, and monk seals live in the Mediterranean Sea, among thousands of other sea creatures.

Life in the Water

Many fish and bird species live in Europe's lakes, rivers, oceans, and seas. The white-tailed eagle is Europe's largest bird of prey. It hunts for fish in the waters of the continent's eastern and northern forests and grasslands.

Cod, herring, halibut, haddock, and mackerel are common fish in northern Europe's salt waters. Small, edible fish called sardines are common in the Mediterranean Sea.

Animals in Trouble

Many of Europe's plant and animal species are in danger of dying out, mainly due to human activities. Here are just a few of them:

Iberian Lynx

Home: Iberian peninsula

This small member of the cat family feeds almost exclusively on rabbits. Only about 400 lynxes remain in Spain and Portugal.

Slender-billed Curlew

Home: Siberian taiga and freshwater habitats around the Mediterranean

It is believed that there are fewer than 50 adult slender-billed curlews left in Europe. These birds were overhunted in the Mediterranean during their winter migrations.

Aeolian Wall Lizard

Home: Aeolian Islands, off the coast of northeastern Sicily

This reptile once possibly roamed all of Italy. Today, there are only about 1,000 of them left in the world.

Mediterranean Monk Seal

Home: Mainly the Mediterranean Sea

Hunting and human settlement along the Mediterranean coast have been the main causes for this seal's near disappearance. It is estimated that there are fewer than 700 Mediterranean monk seals left.

Karpathos Frog

Home: Greece

This amphibian lives near water and areas covered in bushes. Its survival is threatened by the loss of its habitat.

These cave drawings were discovered in 1879. They were made sometime between 14,820 and 13,130 years ago.

The charcoal drawings in the Cave of Altamira in northern Spain portray large bison and other animals.

CHAPTER 3

A Peek at the Past

The direct ancestors of modern Europeans probably began to spread across Europe from northern Africa around 30,000 years ago. These people were skilled hunters, toolmakers, and artists. By about 5,500 BCE, groups of people from the Middle East had also come to Europe. These new arrivals brought farming skills, metal tools, horses, and wheeled carts. They established trade routes between Europe and Asia. By about 4,000 BCE, they lived in organized communities.

Ancient Greece

In about 800 BCE, a very advanced civilization started to develop on the western side of the Mediterranean. These people were the ancient Greeks. They lived in city-states with complex forms of government. They invented democracy, philosophy, architecture, and even the Olympic Games. The Greeks also observed and studied the world. They discovered that Earth was not flat! The ancient Greeks established colonies beyond the Mediterranean Sea. Historians consider the Greeks to be the founders of Western civilization.

Ancient Greeks built temples for their gods and goddesses. The Parthenon, in Athens, was made for Athena, the goddess of war and wisdom. It was completed by 438 BCE.

At the Colosseum, an amphitheater completed in 80 CE, about 50,000 spectators could gather to watch gladiator contests. These were a common and brutal form of entertainment in ancient Rome.

Ancient Rome

The founding of Rome in 753 BCE was the seed of Europe's first great **empire**. For over 1,000 years, Rome ruled large parts of western and southern Europe, including ancient Greece and northern Africa. The Romans brought their culture and their language, Latin, to every place they conquered. To connect their territory, the Romans created an amazing transportation network. The western side of the empire started to collapse in the late 4th century CE, when Germanic tribes from northern Europe invaded.

The Middle Ages

By the end of the 5th century CE, the Western Roman Empire had crumbled. A new era called the Middle Ages began. During this time, Europe was ruled by kings and queens. Many lived in castles and ruled over their serfs. Serfs were usually poor, uneducated farmworkers. Roads fell into disrepair. Trade greatly declined. Cities grew smaller. The Catholic Church had a very important role in society during this time. Between the 11th and 14th centuries, it supported a series of wars called the **Crusades**.

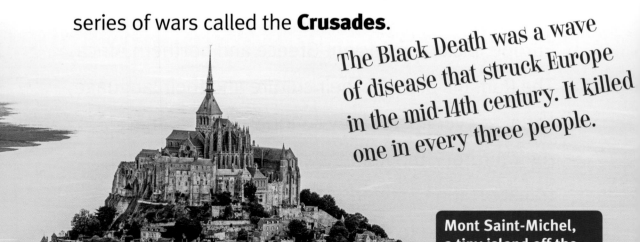

The Black Death was a wave of disease that struck Europe in the mid-14th century. It killed one in every three people.

Mont Saint-Michel, a tiny island off the western coast of France, is crowned by a medieval church.

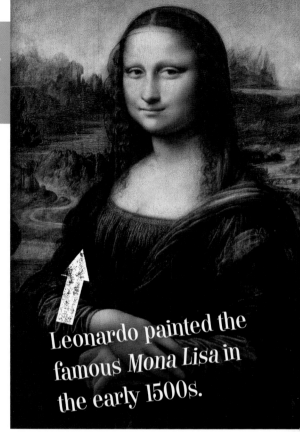

Leonardo painted the famous Mona Lisa in the early 1500s.

Europe's Rebirth

In the 14th century, a new period called the Renaissance began in Italy. The Renaissance brought renewed interest in learning. Art and literature became very important. In 1492, during the Age of Exploration, Italian explorer Christopher Columbus reached America on behalf of the Spanish crown. In 1760, the Industrial Revolution started. Steam was now used to power ships and trains. Industry boomed, and so did city life around the globe. By 1800, Europeans had built empires and colonies across most of the world.

A Century of Change

At the turn of the 20th century, the people of Russia sought new government and better living conditions. The Russian Revolution began in 1917 and led to the creation of the world's first **communist** government. In 1922, Russia formed the Soviet Union, uniting 15 communist republics. During the 20th century, Europe was the setting for two terrible wars: World War I (1914–1918) and World War II (1939–1945).

Timeline of 20th Century Europe

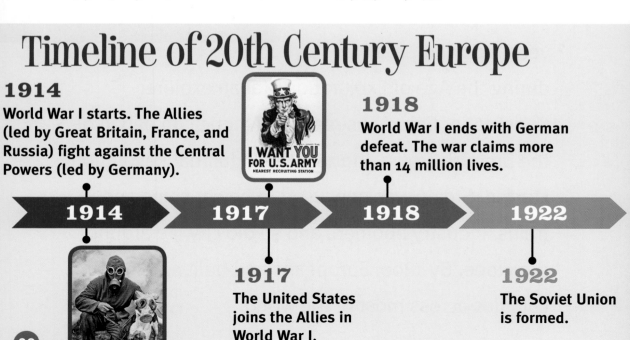

1914
World War I starts. The Allies (led by Great Britain, France, and Russia) fight against the Central Powers (led by Germany).

1918
World War I ends with German defeat. The war claims more than 14 million lives.

1914 | 1917 | 1918 | 1922

1917
The United States joins the Allies in World War I.

1922
The Soviet Union is formed.

After World War II, Europe was divided into two sides. The nations in the west held free elections and were allied with the United States. The eastern nations were communist and supported by the Soviet Union. Their economies and leaders were allied with the Soviet government. This stark division remained until 1989, when the communist governments in Eastern Europe started to collapse.

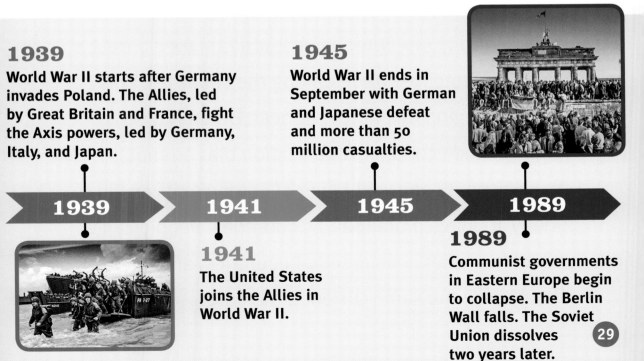

1939
World War II starts after Germany invades Poland. The Allies, led by Great Britain and France, fight the Axis powers, led by Germany, Italy, and Japan.

1945
World War II ends in September with German and Japanese defeat and more than 50 million casualties.

1939 — **1941** — **1945** — **1989**

1941
The United States joins the Allies in World War II.

1989
Communist governments in Eastern Europe begin to collapse. The Berlin Wall falls. The Soviet Union dissolves two years later.

29

In 2016, Great Britain voted to leave the European Union. The process of withdrawal is known as "Brexit."

The egg-shaped center of the Europa Building in Brussels, Belgium, contains meeting rooms where EU officials conduct business.

A New Union

Europe's leaders wanted to prevent tragic events like those of the early 20th century from happening again. In 1957, six European countries signed a treaty that promoted free trade among the countries. This was the beginning of the European Union (EU), a political and economic organization that promotes the prosperity and well-being of Europe's citizens. Today, it unites more than 25 countries. People can travel freely between member countries, and many of them share the same currency, the euro.

The house where Anne Frank went into hiding was later turned into a museum. Her diary is kept there in a special room.

The Diary of a Young Girl

Adolf Hitler was a dictator who sought the expansion of Germany. He had an extreme hatred for Jewish people. During World War II, Germany and its allies murdered at least 6 million Jewish people. This horrible mass murder is known as the Holocaust.

Anne Frank was a Jewish girl who hid with her family during Germany's occupation of the Netherlands. For her thirteenth birthday on June 12,

1942, she was given a blank book. She used it to record her daily experiences. Anne Frank wrote for more than two years, until she was captured and brought to a concentration camp, where she died in 1945. She was only 15 years old.

Her diary was found by her father after the war and published in 1947. It has become a key primary source of the war and has been translated into 60 languages.

Mountains of Garbage

The average EU citizen produces about 3 pounds (1.4 kilograms) of trash each day. Plastic and paper packaging, electronic gadgets, and food scraps pile up to create so much trash that it has become a major problem.

What is the solution to Europe's trash troubles? Many countries in Europe are working to achieve zero waste in the near future! In the meantime, this is how Europeans get rid of all this trash:

Collection
People leave their waste in containers along the street or at home. The trash is then collected by workers.

Incineration

Trash can be burned at special facilities, reducing its bulk by more than 90 percent. However, burning trash can release poisonous fumes that harm the environment.

Landfills

These are giant holes where solid trash is piled and buried. Even if trash is isolated, landfills can leak and hazardous waste can move into the soil, air, and water surrounding it. This harms the environment.

Recycling

This process turns used products into raw materials that can be made into new products. Plastic, glass, metals, paper, and textiles can be recycled. About 44 percent of Europe's waste is recycled. This percentage increases every year.

Export

Europe has also kept itself clean by sending huge amounts of waste to China. However, in 2018, this Asian country passed a law that put restrictions on the import of foreign waste.

Composting

This process turns organic waste into fertilizer, which can be used to help produce crops.

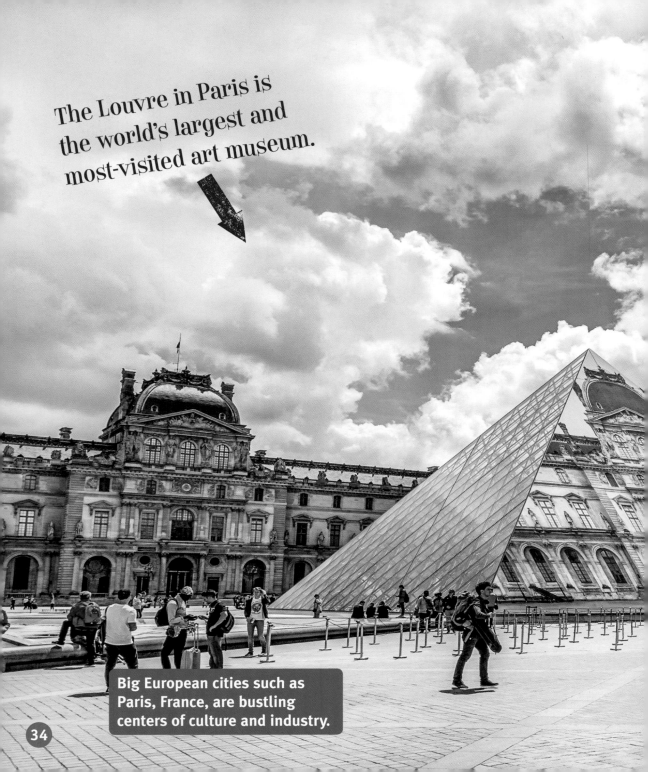

The Louvre in Paris is the world's largest and most-visited art museum.

Big European cities such as Paris, France, are bustling centers of culture and industry.

CHAPTER 4

Europe Today

Language, religion, economic activities, food, and political beliefs can change dramatically from town to town in Europe. There is great cultural diversity among the 742 million people who live in modern Europe's more than 50 countries. However, Europeans are generally very well-educated. Europe's capital cities are connected to each other by high-speed trains and highways. Each of these cities is a vibrant cultural center with rich history. Europe's museums are filled with art, from ancient artifacts to the latest modern works.

Hundreds of thousands of people from Asia and Africa risk their lives every year crossing the Mediterranean Sea trying to make it to Europe.

North and South

In northern Europe, the majority of people are Protestant, though the number of people practicing a religion is decreasing. In southern Europe, the majority are Roman Catholic.

Europe has a decreasing birth rate, and its population is aging. However, many people from diverse ethnic groups have moved to Europe from other continents. Many have brought new religions and customs, contributing to the continent's diversity.

Who's in Charge?

Today, all European nations except for Vatican City have some form of democratic or popularly elected government. This means citizens can vote to elect representatives in open elections. European governments tend to be very involved in the lives of their citizens. Some countries, such as the United Kingdom, also have royal families. Europeans pay high taxes. In return, health insurance and other benefits are provided to all people.

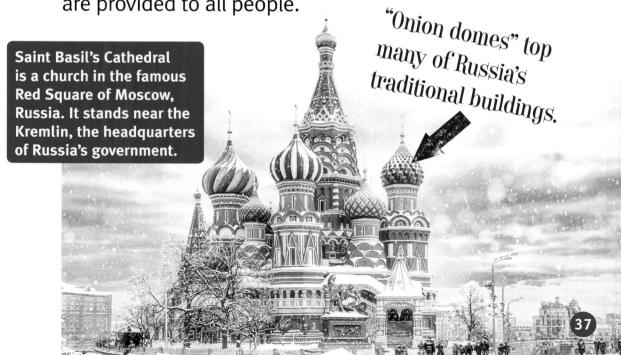

Saint Basil's Cathedral is a church in the famous Red Square of Moscow, Russia. It stands near the Kremlin, the headquarters of Russia's government.

"Onion domes" top many of Russia's traditional buildings.

Ukraine is often called the "breadbasket of Europe" because of its rich soil and vast fields that produce crops.

Economy

Europe has one of the largest economies in the world. It produces and purchases more products and services than any other continent. The economies of 15 western European nations are among the world's 25 strongest. Germany ranks number one. On the other hand, the former communist countries of southeastern Europe tend to have weaker economies. Kosovo, Moldova, and Ukraine are among the poorest countries on the continent.

Made in Europe

An export is a product that a country sells to other nations. This graph shows the top export for each of Europe's four top exporting countries.

Export by Country

Amount Exported in 2016 (in billions of dollars)

Country	Amount
Germany *Cars*	**$154 Billion**
France *Planes, helicopters, spacecraft*	**$49.1 Billion**
Netherlands *Refined petroleum*	**$32.4 Billion**
Italy *Packaged medication*	**$21.8 Billion**

Top Export by Country

Source: MIT Observatory of Economic Complexity

Football and Food

Many sports are played in Europe, but nothing equals the popularity of soccer. Europeans are crazy about this sport, which they call football. The continent's greatest soccer teams, such as FC Barcelona and Bayern München, have fans around the globe.

What's on the menu in Europe? The Mediterranean diet of the south is rich in fresh seafood, beans, and olive oil. In other parts of Europe, red meat, bread, and butter are common. And of course, each region has its own local specialties.

With a capacity of almost 100,000, Camp Nou is the biggest stadium in Europe.

Camp Nou is the home stadium of the FC Barcelona soccer team.

Every August in Buñol, a small town in Spain, people gather to throw around 330,693 pounds (150,000 kg) of old tomatoes at each other in a food fight called La Tomatina.

Time to Celebrate

Celebrations are important in Europe. Easter and Christmas are celebrated in most countries. Muslims throughout Europe observe Ramadan. In Germany, people dress in traditional outfits and enjoy food and drinks during Oktoberfest. In Ireland, St. Patrick's Day is celebrated with huge parades in which the color green is displayed proudly.

Europe is rich in celebrations, history, and culture. It is a vibrant continent that has shaped the world we live in today. ★

Destination

EIFFEL TOWER
France

This iron tower was built in 1889 to celebrate science and engineering achievements of the time. It was the tallest structure in the world until the Chrysler Building was constructed in New York City in 1929.

POMPEII
Italy

Pompeii was once a thriving city of the Roman Empire. In 79 CE, a volcanic eruption covered Pompeii in lava and ash, which preserved the city fo almost 2,000 years. Today, it is open to the public

BERLIN WALL
Germany

In 1961, construction began on a wall to separate the communist and noncommunist sides of Berlin, Germany. A symbol of the Cold War, the wall was torn down in November 1989, but some parts still remain.

MOSCOW SUBWAY
Russia

Thanks to its unique mosaics, sculptures, lamps, and columns, the Moscow subway is widely considered to be the most beautiful subway system in the world. It was opened to the public in 1935, under communist rule.

Europe

VENICE Italy

Venice is the city of water, gondolas, and palaces. It is made up of at least 100 islands connected by canals and bridges.

BUCKINGHAM PALACE United Kingdom

This building of nearly 600 rooms is the London residence of the royal family of the United Kingdom. The symbolic changing of the guard ceremony takes place several times a day.

VATICAN CITY

This small country stands in the middle of the city of Rome and is ruled by the pope, the leader of the Catholic Church. It is home to the world's second-largest church, Saint Peter's Basilica, as well as some of the world's finest works of art.

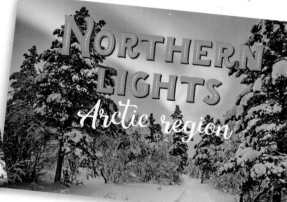

NORTHERN LIGHTS Arctic region

When particles from the sun enter Earth's atmosphere in the Arctic, they create these beautiful colorful lights in the sky. The northern lights are also known as aurora borealis.

43

Length of the Volga River, Europe's longest river: 2,193 miles (3,529 km)

Height of Russia's Mount Elbrus, Europe's tallest mountain: 18,510 feet (5,642 m)

Number of time zones that spanned the Soviet Union, the world's largest country for much of the 20th century: 11

Number of European countries with royal families: 10

Number of broken ancient Roman olive oil containers that form Italy's Monte Testaccio: 25 million

Age of these containers: More than 2,000 years

Did you find the truth?

T Soccer is the most popular sport in Europe.

F The Olympic Games were invented by the Ancient Romans.

Resources

Books

Baxter, Roberta. *Learning About Europe.* Minneapolis: Lerner Publishing Group, Inc., 2016.

Eamer, Claire. *What a Waste! Where Does Garbage Go?* Toronto: Annick Press, 2017.

Gifford, Clive. *Europe: Everything You Ever Wanted to Know.* Victoria, Australia: Lonely Planet, 2013.

Spilsbury, Louise, and Richard Spilsbury. *Animals in Danger in Europe.* Chicago: Heinemann Library, 2013.

Williams, Rachel. *Atlas of Adventures.* New York: Wide Eyed Editions, 2015.

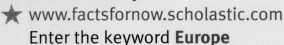

Visit this Scholastic website for more information on Europe:

⭐ www.factsfornow.scholastic.com
Enter the keyword **Europe**

Important Words

communist (KAHM-yoo-nist) relating to a way of organizing the economy of a country so that all of the land, property, businesses, and resources belong to the government or community, and the profits are shared by all

Crusades (kroo-SADEZ) the battles fought during the 11th, 12th, and 13th centuries by European Christians attempting to capture biblical lands from the Muslims

empire (EM-pire) a group of countries or states that have the same ruler

erosion (ih-ROH-zhuhn) the wearing away of something by water or wind

habitat (HAB-ih-tat) the place where an animal or a plant is usually found

inlets (IN-lets) narrow bodies of water that lead inland from a larger body of water, such as an ocean

latitudes (LAT-ih-toodz) measurements of distance north or south of the equator

migratory (MYE-gruh-tor-ee) relating to animals or people that move from one area or climate to another at particular times of year

peninsula (puh-NIN-suh-luh) a piece of land that sticks out from a larger landmass and is almost completely surrounded by water

Index

Page numbers in **bold** indicate illustrations.

About the Author

Joana Costa Knufinke is originally from Barcelona, a beautiful European city on the Mediterranean coast. Her mother is German, and Joana started traveling around the continent to visit her family when she was young. So far, she has set foot in 24 European countries. Joana holds a master's degree in literature from the University of Barcelona and a master's degree in publishing from New York University, which she obtained thanks to a Fulbright scholarship. She currently works as an editor at Scholastic, and she lives in New York City with her family. She can order food in six different European languages!